Bridge Pag

Bridge Pages

B. Vincent

Published by RWG Publishing, 2021.

BRIDGE PAGES

First edition. June 16, 2021.

Written by B. Vincent.

Also by B. Vincent

Bridge Pages
Marketing Automation

Table of Contents

Module 1

Welcome to Module One. In this module, our expert will cover the overall bridge page concept. So, get ready to take some notes. And let's jump right in.

ALRIGHT, FOLKS, SO let's lay the groundwork for what a bridge page is, and why you might want to use one. So, with traditional non-email affiliate marketing, you generally be doing something like the following, you'd go out there and you choose an affiliate offer, you get your link for it. And then you go create content on the web, or you pay for ads, all with the intention of driving traffic to your affiliate link, and to that offer, right. And then you'd sit back in hopes of making some sales and commissions from at least a small percentage of that traffic. Traffic that you worked really hard and really long for, or that you spent a good chunk of money on. And that last part, there is the concern that led to the development of the bridge page concept. You see, if you're sending traffic directly from your traffic sources, and remember, this is non-email traffic we're talking about, if you're sending traffic directly to the offer, you're basically wasting a ton of effort, or money. Even if you're making sales and even if you're profitable with those campaigns, there's still so much left on the table that you can never get back.

1

Because the vast majority of that traffic that you worked so hard to produce and to drive will not buy. We already know that, right? The vast majority of people will go to a sales page and leave without buying, they'll leave the offer page and you'll never see them again. And the idea behind the bridge page is that's your traffic, you worked hard for it, you put in the hours or the effort creating content to drive it or you invested your money to pay for that traffic. So, it's not right that 97% of it should just disappear off into the [sp] ether.

Now with a bridge page, you maintain a positive control of that traffic initially. And you capture a large percentage of those people of those visitors as leads before redirecting them to the offer. You add them to your email list, to your tribe so that you can then market to them later, market to them with follow up emails, sort of re encouraging them to buy that particular offer that you were promoting in that campaign. And market to them forever with as many relevant offers as you want for as long as they stay on your list. Does that kind of make sense? It's your traffic paid for either with money or effort, and you deserve to have more chances later on to monetize it. So that's why this whole bridge page concept exists. And your list is arguably your most important asset. If you invested to drive traffic, then a good chunk of that traffic should end up on your list. So, let's see what the bridge page operation actually looks like when you map it out. So, here's your traffic, let's say it's from paid ads, or YouTube videos, or whatever. And over here is the affiliate offer that you've chosen to promote, and that you have an affiliate link for. And rather than sending your traffic directly to that link and to that offer, you stick this page in the middle. This is the page that you send your traffic to. And on this page, you basically offer something of value and return for them typing in their email address. And you set up the page and the email, opt in form in a way that it then redirects them after they filled out the form. It redirects them to your affiliate link for that affiliate offer. So, boom, you've captured leads and you're instantly monetizing those leads by directing them to the affiliate link. Does that kind of make sense?

Now, there's a couple of different ways to do this, and varying opinions on the best way. And number one is the totally minimal hands off less friction method. That's what we'll call it for our purposes here. And this method you do and say barely anything on the bridge page, you have like one headline maybe about what you're sending them to like—let's say the affiliate offer is for a video creation software. And the headline might say, want to see the easiest video creator ever made? And then there's the email address, or the form or the button which brings up the email address and a lightbox or pop up, which is probably the more common type of landing page that you see today. Not a lot of words, not a lot of images, not a lot of branding, right. And that's it, they see that headline and they click the button, submit their email address and then boom, you send them off to the offer.

Now the argument here is that the less you do and show and say on that page, The higher your OPT in rate will be, the more likely people are to convert and join your list. And there is some truth to that, generally speaking, the less friction there is on a page, the less things to read and look at and the simpler it is, the higher your conversion rate will be. That's a general rule, it doesn't always apply but it applies in many cases. However, you have to ask yourself, what have you just done when someone does in fact, go through that process? You've just added someone to your email list who has no idea who you or your company are, no idea about your brand or anything, and probably doesn't realize that they joined your list. Meaning when they get to that affiliate offer page, they probably assume that the email form that they just filled out was for the same guy or company who's making the offer. Which makes logical sense, right? So, when you send them a marketing email after that, if you use this method, the minimalist approach, when you send them a marketing email later, what are they going to think? They'll have no idea who you are, they'll have no idea that they joined your list or why you're bugging them. And what are you going to say in that welcome sequence? Thanks for putting in your email and letting me forward you to another business. Thanks for giving me your email in return for nothing from me. You see what I mean? There's no context for it. It doesn't make any logical sense. And in fact, it's likely to make people angry and irritated. As a result, it's likely your open rates will be low, your click throughs will be low, your affinity and your trust with this list are going to be low, your spam rate and your unsubscribe rate will be high, which all together, all that stuff combined will lead generally to a lower deliverability. Not to mention a potentially bad reputation. In other words, you could be creating a much less profitable list this way, a list that might be numerically superior because of a higher conversion rate, so more emails but less profitable.

And that's just one of many opinions. There are people out there who really liked this method and people who don't like it. Arguably, the more profitable method would be method number two, which is what we call the relevant angle method. And what this means is you do for yourself or your brand out there a little on your bridge page, and you do a little bit of talking and messaging on that bridge page. Specifically, not too much. But specifically, you come up with some sort of relevant free offer that directly ties into your affiliate offer that you're sending them to, you tie whatever this is, it has to be tied in with the offer that you're about to redirect them to in a reasonable and coherent way. And it's important to clearly mention on that page that you're going to be sending them this gift via email right now. And then you ensure obviously, that you have an initial autoresponder email sequence, welcome emails that effectively remind them about when they signed up. Because you see, after they opt in and get redirected from your bridge page, they're going to be going through that affiliate offer funnel, they're going to be going through someone else's funnel, they're going to be exposed to someone else's brand, someone else's name and face and story and videos and message and you get the idea, they're going to be exposed to all that. And it's probably going to be lengthy, which means they're going to have forgotten about you, at least a little bit. And you need to refresh their memory in that initial email, they need to be reminded of that moment when they were on your page, your bridge page, they don't know that it's a bridge page obviously. But when they were on your page, and they need to be made conscious of the fact that there's a distinction between you and the other person or company that they saw afterwards, the affiliate offer that you sent them to. And that they're also getting value from you separately, value which they chose to say yes to and which as you promise you're now delivering in this initial email.

So, all that's very important to do in those initial emails. And then that makes sure that you've got a solid sequence of at least two or three more emails designed to sort of welcome indoctrinate and solidify that relationship between you and your list. This method stands a much higher chance of building a list of leads who will actually expect your emails, open your emails and know, like and trust you, which means less spam, complaints, less unsubscribes, healthier, deliverability, and so on and so forth. So some would argue that even if method number one, the minimalist, less friction method, even if that does in fact have a higher conversion rate than the relevant angle method that we just got done talking about, it's still better to go with the ladder, because it'll likely far make up in lead quality, what it lacks in initial conversion rates, because the quality of the list and the relationship and the trust and the open rates and all that stuff really matters, it'll still cause a slightly smaller list to outperform a slightly larger list that lacks all of those important elements. So now that we understand the idea, the overall concept and the intricacies of the bridge page method, let's move on to the next lesson, which will cover actually finding a product to promote and brainstorming an angle for our bridge page.

Module 2

Hey, folks, welcome to Module Two. In this module, our expert will cover determining the offer and the angle, so get ready to take some notes. And let's jump right in.

Alright, so like we discussed at the end of the last video, the relevant angle approach to bridge pages is arguably the superior way because of the higher quality list, more trust and affinity with your audience, and so on and so forth. And so, what we're going to do in this video, it'll be pretty short, we're just going to go through and look at a bunch of different offers, affiliate offers that we could promote. And we're going to try and come up with where I brainstorm and hypothesize and just sort of come up with an idea of an angle that we could create for a bridge page for that product. So, let's jump right into, let's say, the E-business, e-marketing niche here on the Click bank marketplace. Let's just see what we got going on here. So, we've got, let's see perpetual income, 365, home business offer. Sounds interesting, but I'm looking for something that jumps out at us right away, very clear how we could create an angle for us, I don't really know what that product is based on the name of it. So just for brevity's sake, let's look at the obvious ones. Let's see, the 12-minute affiliate system hot offer. Who else wants to make 50% commissions, etc., etc.? Okay, so let's just use this one as an example here. Just off the top of my head, let's say that this is obviously a product that includes a special system or method for how to do affiliate marketing. So, let's say that we came up with and created a list of existing affiliate offers on Click bank, warrior plus JVZoo, that have good solid sales history and performance. And we compiled those into a PDF document listing, let's say, 10 top products that you can be an affiliate for that you have good conversion rates. That would be actually pretty easy to do, we could create that. And that would be a useful little resource for people, a useful little PDF, let's say the headline was—remember, a bridge page, relatively minimalist but we put our message and our branding out there a little bit. So maybe a picture of you. And then the headline says, let me show you the hottest 12-minute affiliate system of 2020, or whatever. So, your one headline, obviously refers to the offer that you're about to redirect them to. And then underneath that, plus, let me hand you the top 10 most lucrative affiliate products to promote right now. Something along those lines. Now, I just made that up off the top of my head on the spot. So that's not going to be your best copy to use on the sales page per se. But you get the idea. So, you've got the product, we've got something that we could easily create that is our own that we could give to them a value so that they opt into our list on the bridge page. And we can deliver that via email and remember, why they received it from us and why they're on our email list? While at the same time remaining totally relevant and coherence with the offer, this offer here that we are going to redirect them to afterwards.

So that's just one example. Let's see here, scribble is the world's number one eBook creator. This, if I recall, is just a software that makes it really quick and easy to format and crank out eBooks. So, an easy one here would be, if we have PLR. Not PLR where we acquired the PLR license but rather PLR of our own, where we give other people the PLR license. We could add that here easy. So how about we show you. The top headline on the bridge page could be something along the lines of—like, we're going to show you the world's number one eBook creator. Get creative with your copy. Something along the lines of, you've never seen an eBook created this fast. And you're kind of teasing it, because they got to opt in to go see the video. But relevant angle method, we could also say, plus, will literally hand you 10 fully written eBooks to use with the software, and then make yourself the author, something along those lines. So that would be a relevant offer to put on a bridge page for scribble. And you could easily do that in a very coherent, relevant, smooth way and gain some quality leads that way. Let's see here, sale who? Wholesale drop ship directory. Extremely high number of niche keywords, you can promote [inaudible 16:14] So it's a drop ship wholesale directory. So, this presumably, is a product where if you want to stock your Shopify store with drop shippable products, here's a directory where you can just go right in and grab them. So that sounds pretty cool. So, an angle for this one might be, let's say, maybe a PDF report of the top 10 physical products to dropship. The top 10 drop shipping, or most profitable drop shipping products of 2020, something along those lines. So, you're getting the idea here, commission hero, same thing, I think, as the affiliate system up here, 12-minute affiliate system, you could create something really quick, really easy that it doesn't take a whole lot of time, or expertise or money on your part to create it, but it does provide some value. And you can hand that to people on the bridge page you're having to do with, the top affiliate offers that they can promote or something along those lines. Same story for a lot of these things, it's relatively easy to come up with a small free gift type informational product that you can hand over on the bridge page, and make your marketing relatively relevant and coherent.

Let's head over to google.com real quick, and let's stick with—I like this idea, just for our example, Let's stick with the drop shipping idea. So, let's head over to google.com. Let's see if we can find some type of say, top drop shipping products. And what we're looking for here is content, publicly available content that we could utilize to sort of curate or compile into a report. So, this looks like an interesting article here over at [sp 18:23]. So, women's shapewear, there's some trends here and some data that prove that is a happening and trending product. Animals slash novelty socks. Okay, very cool. Some data there. Baby hip seats, That's interesting, right there. Let's see some data. Because you wouldn't want to just create like a random conjecture or opinion piece that you offer as a gift because that's not as valuable. This is good stuff here because we actually see numbers backing it up. So, we know that we're actually handing over some actual, truthful and useful information. Interactive pet toys, very cool. So, we could go out there and find a few blog posts like this, articles like this that talk about the top trending ecommerce drop shipping products and compile those into our own list in a PDF, a very short minimalist list that hits all the main points of all these and combines maybe a handful of each of the products from each of these blog posts and articles into our top 10 lists And we could do that relatively easily, it might take half an hour Alright, now we've created something that's valuable, that we can give away for free to potential leads who come to our bridge page before we send them off to the affiliate offer. Obviously, if you're going to be curating content and content ideas, never actually copy and paste and take someone else's intellectual property. We're talking about coming in here and just using this as research and inspiration. And obviously, throughout your report, make sure you're citing and referencing the original sources and the appropriate ways, ethical with your content creation. But we could easily slap that onto a PDF and then upload and host that somewhere and then create our bridge page and set it up so that remember, once they opt in and say yes, we immediately do two things. First, we redirect them to the affiliate offer, which in this case was that drop shipping offer here, sale who, wholesale and dropship directory. And at the same time in the background, we're sending them that email. Again, an autoresponder sequence, we're sending them that email. And in that email, we remind them of that moment when they just opted in so that they don't forget about us. We welcome them to the tribe and we deliver the product as promised and that sort of thing, and you start nurturing that lead. But first, we got to create the actual page that we're going to stick between your traffic and the affiliate offer. We got to create that bridge page and that's what we're going to do moving on to the next lesson.

Module 3

All right, welcome to Module Three. In this module, our expert will show you how to actually build the page itself. So, get ready to take some notes. And let's jump right in.

Alright, so here we are the third and final piece of the puzzle, creating the actual bridge page. Okay, so we're going to be using Instapage to create this page. Nice and drag and drop simple. We'll go ahead and start with a blank page and create this from scratch. We'll call this bridge. And here we are in the editor. So, what we can do here is, first, we'll pick a background color. So, let's maybe make this more of the darker variety. Black won't grab up, background image. And let's say maybe—here we go. Good old, stereotypical training image. Doesn't really matter what the details of the image are, because we're going to be adding an overlay that will make it barely visible. Really, the main point of this is just to make it look like it's not just 100% solid black. It just adds another layer of 'interestiness' to the page for the visitors. There we go, 91% that should work just fine. And we can if we like we're going to set a parallax effect so it stays stationary as the page scrolls up and down. And let's see, let's start with a headline. Headline, I will make that a white. And if you'll recall, what we are ultimately promoting is a drop shipping directory product. So, let's see if we can craft a clever headline here. How about something along the lines of what if you instantly had hundreds of the world's drop shipping suppliers at your fingertips? Let's try that. All caps for the headline. There we go. So pretty short, sweet to the point headline. Let's go ahead and stretch that out a little bit, bigger and increase the text size. So, there's our main headline. And then what we can stick under that is literally just a plus sign or we put the word plus. And let's say bright red to bring their attention to the additional gift that we're going to be adding. And the gift that we were going to be adding was basically a PDF report that details the top 10 most profitable drop shipping products based on current trends at this time. So, let's say Ctrl C, Ctrl V will make this one a little bit smaller. Let's see, how about plus. 'We're surely going to hand you the top 10 most profitable products to the dropship right now'. Let's make this a little bit smaller. Let's put 'right now' in bright red and let's put the 'hand you' bright red and underline that. Oops, didn't mean to do that. There we go.

Alright, so what if you instantly had the world's dropship suppliers at your fingertips? And you know a second thought? I hate to go back and forth in this lesson here, but it's good idea to brainstorm different ideas and stuff. This was looking a little bit wordy. I say let's change it up. How about, "Would you like to access the [27:59] world's number one drop shipping database?" There we go, I think is a little bit more appropriate. And next step is going to be to add a form. Okay, let's get rid of this section up here. Now, typically, these days, what you see more often is people will have a button by itself with no form and that leads into a lightbox, a lightbox or a pop up. So that's what we'll do here. Let's go ahead and make our Button Red and the hover color for when the mouse is over, like that kind of a darker red. Can't see it here only happens in the preview. And let's see here, text is white. Let's go ahead and make the button text, how about, "Yes, send it to me!"? Actually, on their mind, we want them to be focusing on this one here since the sending is actually going to be us emailing that to them via their autoresponder sequence. And we want them to remember that they're going to be getting something from us. They'll be redirected to the main offer after this but we really want to make sure they remember that they'll be getting something in their inbox from us. So, we've got the button There. Let's go ahead and delete this here. We can expand the page a little bit.

Okay, now the next step here would be to create that lightbox that we talked about. And the whole point behind this is basically a principle called micro commitment. The idea is when people show up to a page, the first thing they see is an email address form, they're going to get spooked, that they're not going to like the fact that they have to put in their email address on a page. Whereas if they don't see that when they show up, they're still intrigued, and they'll read the headline and stick around for a few seconds. And then once they click the button, they've already said yes to something, would you like this report on drop shipping? They're clicking yes and psychologically that kind of commits them towards that. It's them convincing themselves that they want this. And they've already gone one step clicking. So, they might as well fill out the email form. Sounds goofy but it really does work that way. It's been proven time and time again in many split tests that that phenomenon works. It doesn't necessarily mean that it will always work better than having a form on the page. You've always got to split test things, things change, people's behavior and psychology changes. But it certainly seems as though the light box approach, the micro commitment approach usually wins out. Let's go ahead and drop a form here. And I want to make sure everything looks congruent with the rest of the page. So, we'll go ahead and change the color here to a red just like our other button. Same thing here, the button text will say, 'send to me'. And we'll make that nice bold email and name. And above that will have a little headline that says, before we show you the directory—let me call that super directory, just to make it sound a little bit more interesting. Because directory is not a very exciting word, we'll email you your top 10 drop shipping products. So that's the text. Now, let's format a little better. See, color to white. Edit, make that center. There we go, stick that right there. Let's go ahead and put, we'll email you in a red because we want them to remember that later. They're expecting us and we can have that healthier, more trusting relationship with our list.

So that is the headline form here. Yeah, that's about it. Now let's go over here to submission. And this is where we figure out what we want to do after they hit Submit on the form. This is very important. What we want to do is we'll come back over here to Click bank, come over here to sale-who, wholesale on dropship directory, we're going to click promote 50% commission, generate hop links, copy our hotlink there. Good, good, good. Come back over here and right over here in the right-hand side, the form submission results in a redirect, not a download but a redirect to an outside URL. And that's where we paste our affiliate link. Okay guys, hit save and boom, done and done. So, here's our quite cool looking still minimalist page that makes it very Clear big idea, big deal out of the fact that we're going to be handing them the top 10 most profitable products to dropship. And you could personalize this, you could stick you face or remove the background, PNG image of you somewhere on here, or your logo at the top, that sort of thing. Don't be afraid to incorporate your branding a little bit so that you're fighting for that real estate in their memory, in their mind, so that they remember you when you start emailing them. So don't be afraid to do that, you don't have to do too much. The really important thing here is that you make it clear that you are going to be emailing them something so that they're expecting something from you and you get that higher quality list. But that's our bridge page. That's how you set it up. That's how we redirect it. And that's how we give those folks some value while adding them to our list before we monetize them. And we make sure that we get to retain and benefit from the traffic that we spent time, effort and or money providing and driving. Alright guys, hope that was useful to you guys, and I wish you the best of luck.

Hello, and welcome to this course on Bridge Page Marketing. In this course, we're going to cover how to generate leads and make sales using bridge pages. This course is divided into three modules. Module One covers the overall bridge page concept, module two covers determining the offer and the angle, and module three shows us how to actually build the page itself. By the time this course is over, you'll know how to effectively leverage bridge pages for your business. So, without further ado, let's dive into the first module.

Don't miss out!

Visit the website below and you can sign up to receive emails whenever B. Vincent publishes a new book. There's no charge and no obligation.

https://books2read.com/r/B-A-QWUO-DGPPB

BOOKS 2 READ

Connecting independent readers to independent writers.

Also by B. Vincent

Affiliate Marketing
Affiliate Marketing
Affiliate Marketing

Standalone
Affiliate Recruiting
Business Layoffs & Firings
Business and Entrepreneur Guide
Business Remote Workforce
Career Transition
Project Management
Precision Targeting
Professional Development
Strategic Planning
Content Marketing
Imminent List Building
Getting Past GateKeepers
Banner Ads
Bookkeeping

Bridge Pages
Marketing Automation

About the Publisher

Accepting manuscripts in the most categories. We love to help people get their words available to the world.

Revival Waves of Glory focus is to provide more options to be published. We do traditional paperbacks, hardcovers, audio books and ebooks all over the world. A traditional royalty-based publisher that offers self-publishing options, Revival Waves provides a very author friendly and transparent publishing process, with President Bill Vincent involved in the full process of your book. Send us your manuscript and we will contact you as soon as possible.

Contact: Bill Vincent at rwgpublishing@yahoo.com www.rwgpublishing.com